Outlines for Christmas Sermons

John S. Meyer

BAKER BOOK HOUSE
Grand Rapids, Michigan

Contents

1. The Battle of the Ages 3
2. God's Call to Abraham 4
3. Until Shiloh Comes 5
4. The Still Small Voice 6
5. God with Us 7
6. His Name Is Wonderful 8
7. The Shoot out of the Stump of Jesse 8
8. Good News for the Weak 9
9. The Tree out of Dry Ground 10
10. Great Advent Prophecies: His Birthplace 12
11. That Beautiful Name 13
12. How Wise Men Listen to God 14
13. Three Reactions to Christmas 15
14. Why the Wise Men Were Wise 16
15. Home for the Holidays 17
16. The Forerunner's Mother 18
17. Fear Not, Zechariah! 19
18. The Christmas Angel 20
19. The Miraculous Birth 21
20. The "Magnificat" 22
21. The "Benedictus" 23
22. The Dayspring from on High 24
23. The Faces of the Shepherds 25
24. The Message Heard by the Shepherds 26
25. Fear Not, Shepherds 27
26. The Sign Received by the Shepherds 28
27. The Paradox of Christ's Coming: Peace or Sword? ... 28
28. The Child Found by the Shepherds 30
29. The Witness of the Shepherds 31
30. The Worship Expressed by the Shepherds 32
31. The Problem of Post-Christmas Blues 33
32. The "Nunc Dimittis" 34
33. The Miracle of Christmas 35
34. Why Jesus Came 36
35. The Paradox of Christ's Coming:
    To Judge or Not to Judge 37
36. The Universal Longing 38
37. What Time Is It? 39
38. Advent Hope 40
39. In the Fullness of Time 41
40. A Lesson in Humility 42
    APPENDIX: Five Series of Advent Messages 43

Copyright 1980 by
Baker Book House Company
ISBN: 0-8010-6107-5

Fifth printing, September 1988

1

The Battle of the Ages

Genesis 3:15

The very first promise in Scripture concerning the coming of the Messiah points to a battle which would not be complete until Christ's victory on the cross.

I. The Origin of the Battle
   A. The fall of man into sin
      1. Satan won the initial skirmish
         a. He tempted Eve
         b. He caused them to eat forbidden fruit
         c. There followed a sense of shame and sin
         d. God came looking for Adam and Eve
         e. God spoke these words to Satan
      2. Satan did not win the war; God pronounced judgment on Satan
   B. The result of the fall into sin—enmity
      1. A new relationship with Satan was established by the fall
      2. God would not allow this new relationship to continue
      3. God established a spirit of enmity
      4. *Enmity* is really a word of "grace"
         a. It was a result of sin
         b. It was God's act of separation

II. The Opponents in the Battle
   A. Initially—the serpent and the woman
   B. Later—the seed of the serpent and the seed of the woman
   C. Ultimately—Christ and Satan
   D. Today—there is still a struggle between good and evil

III. The Outcome of the Battle
   A. He (Christ) shall crush the head of the serpent
   B. The serpent shall bruise His heel
   C. This is a promise of victory
   D. It was fulfilled in the birth, life, and death of Christ

Conclusion

2

God's Call to Abraham

Genesis 12:1-3

God continued the movement toward Christmas by calling one man, Abraham, out of his native land, leading him to a new country, giving him numerous promises, and assuring him that one day the entire world would be blessed in him.

I. **God's Command Stated**
   A. Move out
   B. A new land
   C. Be thou a blessing
      1. Abraham's missionary mandate
      2. God's purpose
         a. Not isolation
         b. But to reach out and be a blessing

II. **God's Promise Given**
   A. A great nation
   B. Great prosperity
   C. Great name
   D. Great influence ("in you shall all the families of the earth be blessed")
      1. The promise referred to the coming Messiah
      2. The promise was given in the family context
      3. The promise was universal in scope

III. **God's Promise Fulfilled**
   A. It is constantly repeated
      1. Genesis 18:18
      2. Genesis 22:18
      3. Genesis 26:2—to Isaac
      4. Genesis 28:14—to Jacob
   B. It is frequently quoted
      1. Acts 3:25
      2. Galatians 3:8
   C. It is long-awaited
   D. It is Christ-centered
      1. Christmas is the "blessing for the world" promised to Abraham

2. Christmas makes all believers children of Abraham (cf. Gal. 3:29)

Conclusion
Abraham teaches us how to live in:
Faith—Hebrews 11:8–9
Patience—Hebrews 11:9
Obedience—Genesis 22:18

3

Until Shiloh Comes

Genesis 49:10

Ruling authority would belong to the tribe of Judah until the coming of the Messiah, after which the authority would belong to Him.

Introduction:
This is the first time the Messiah is named in Scripture.
The name is Shiloh.
Where did Jacob get this name?
Possibly at the time of wrestling with the angel years earlier.

I. The Preeminence of Judah
   A. Why was Judah singled out?
      1. Reuben bypassed because of sin (49:4)
      2. Simeon and Levi bypassed because of hot temper (vv.5–7)
      3. Judah was chosen
         a. Name means "The Lord be praised"
         b. He was an instrument of healing in his family
         c. Ultimately it was God's choice (election)
   B. How long did Judah have this preeminence?
      1. Until Shiloh comes
      2. Line of Christ came through David from Judah
      3. All tribal lines were lost after A.D. 70
      4. Shiloh had to be Jesus Christ

II. The Preeminence of Christ
   A. In the name *Shiloh* (often left untranslated) two possibilities:
      1. Means "the one to whom it (sceptre and ruler's staff) belongs"; implication: power and kingly authority

2. Means "the rest-giver" or "prince of peace"; Shiloh was the place where the tabernacle later stood
   3. First meaning is better
  B. In the obedience He deserves
   1. It is spontaneous obedience
   2. It is rooted in godly piety
  C. In the Christmas fulfillment (birth of Christ)
   1. Jesus Christ is Lord and God
   2. Jesus Christ is our King
  D. In the consummation of His kingdom at the last day
   1. Rev. 5:5 "the lion of the tribe of Judah has overcome"
   2. The lion overcame by becoming the Lamb of God

Conclusion

4

The Still Small Voice

I Kings 19:11–12

When the despondent Elijah ran off into the wilderness hoping to die, God came down and revealed Himself to the prophet, not in the spectacular elements of nature, but in a still small voice.

I. The Need for this Revelation
  A. Elijah's depression
   1. Caused by weariness
   2. Caused by letdown
   3. Caused by loneliness
  B. Elijah's fear
   1. Caused by threats to his life
   2. Caused him to run away and hide

II. The Method of Revelation
  A. Negatively
   1. God was not in the wind
   2. God was not in the earthquake
   3. God was not in the fire
  B. Positively—the still small voice
   1. God is in the still and gentle influences of life

    2. God is in the small and unspectacular events of life
    3. God speaks through a voice
    4. God was preparing the way for the still small voice of the babe in the manger
III. **The Result of the Revelation**
    A. Elijah was told to go back to work (vv.15–16)
    B. Elijah was given words of assurance (v.18)
    C. Elijah was told to prepare to be replaced (vv.19–21)
Conclusion

5

God with Us

Isaiah 7:14 and Matthew 1:23

Isaiah's mysterious birth announcement directs our attention to the great miracle of Christmas.

I. **The Mystery of the Announcement**
    A. Meaning of the word "almah"
        1. Virgin or young woman
        2. Almah vs. Betheulah
    B. Meaning of the word "sign"
        1. The problem that emerges
            a. Was it the birth itself?
            b. Was it the birth before the destruction of the two kingdoms?
        2. A second problem that emerges
            a. The sign was for King Ahaz
            b. More distant fulfillment for New Testament age
II. **The Miracle of the Virgin Birth**
    A. Matthew's use of this prophecy
    B. Matthew points to the supernatural birth of Christ
    C. Implications of this miracle
        1. Jesus Christ is both human and divine
        2. Jesus Christ is without sin
III. **The Meaning of Redemption**
    A. What "Immanuel" meant for King Ahaz

    B. What "Immanuel" means for us today
       1. God with us
       2. Redemption through Jesus Christ

Conclusion

6

His Name Is Wonderful

Isaiah 9:6

Christmas marks the birth of a wonderful savior.

I. Christ Is Wonderful in His Birth
    A. He is God's gift to us
    B. He is an unusual gift
       1. He is man ("unto us a child is born")
       2. He is God ("unto us a Son is given")

II. Christ Is Wonderful in His Task
    A. He is a King who governs
    B. He is a King who bears all the weight of government

III. Christ Is Wonderful in His Names
    A. Wonderful Counselor
    B. The mighty God
    C. The everlasting Father
    D. The Prince of Peace

Conclusion

7

The Shoot out of the Stump of Jesse

Isaiah 11:1–10

Jesus Christ is the shoot out of the stump of Jesse.

I. **His Amazing Birth (v.1)**
   A. Background—the fall of the Assyrian dynasty in chapter 10
   B. Jesus is a descendent of David (Jesse)
      1. Promises of II Samuel 7:13–14
      2. Psalm 89:6
      3. Isaiah 9:7
   C. Jesus will come at a time of humiliation for the line of David
      1. The line will be intact
      2. But it will be like a great tree cut down with only a stump left
   D. Jesus will bear much fruit

II. **His Spiritual Resources (v.2)**
   A. Jesus' intellectual life ("Spirit of wisdom and understanding")
   B. Jesus' practical ability ("Spirit of counsel and might")
   C. Jesus spiritual life ("Spirit of knowledge and fear of the Lord")

III. **His Great Task (vv.3–5)**
   A. His delight shall be in the fear of the Lord
   B. He shall judge the poor with righteousness
   C. He shall deal with the meek in fairness
   D. He shall smite the earth in judgment

IV. **His Long-Range Goals (vv.6–10)**
   A. The restoration of nature
   B. The earth filled with the knowledge of the Lord
   C. The nations of the world attracted to Him

Conclusion

8

Good News for the Weak

Isaiah 42:1–4 and Matthew 12:17–20

God's servant, the Christ of Christmas, will gently and tenderly carry on His work of bringing justice to the nations of this world.

I. **The Picture of Human Weakness**
    A. Like a bruised reed
    B. Like a smoking flax
II. **The Prophecy of God's Son Meeting This Need**
    A. His servant nature
        1. One of several "servant" passages in Isaiah (cf. Isa. 53)
        2. He is upheld by God
        3. He is chosen by God
        4. He is the one God delights in (cf. Jesus' baptism)
    B. His saving work
        1. He is full of God's spirit
        2. He promotes justice for the Gentiles
        3. He brings "right living" to the nations
    C. His quiet humility
        1. He does not draw attention to Himself
            a. His quiet birth
            b. His humble life
        2. He works with compassion and love toward the weak
            a. He does not break the bruised reed
            b. He does not quench the dim wick
        3. He demonstrates this compassion in his healing ministry (cf. Matt. 12:17–20)
    D. His ultimate success
        1. He will not fail
        2. He will not be discouraged
        3. Justice to the world
        4. His law to the isles of the sea

Conclusion

9

The Tree out of Dry Ground

Isaiah 53:1–3

Isaiah portrays Jesus as a young tree whose roots grow out of dry ground.

I. Isaiah's Picture of Jesus
   A. His humble origin
      1. Like a root out of dry ground
      2. Line of David was dry and barren
      3. Jesus' earthly parents were poor and humble

   B. His growth and development
      1. Like a tender plant
      2. Born as a baby
      3. Grew up in obscurity
      4. Unnoticed by the world
      5. But noticed by God ("grew up before Him")

   C. His unattractive form
      1. He has no form nor comeliness
      2. Jesus was not dashing or alluring
      3. Jesus lived a plain and simple life
      4. He had no special beauty or handsome features

   D. His rejection by men
      1. He was despised and rejected
      2. Rejection came at the hands of men of learning and culture

   E. His sorrow of heart
      1. He was a man of sorrows
         a. A stranger in a strange land
         b. A life full of sorrow and suffering
      2. He was acquainted with grief
         a. Literally, "acquainted with sicknesses"
         b. He had compassion on the sick and suffering
      3. He was not esteemed by men
         a. He was not making His way to a throne
         b. He was making His way to a cross

II. Isaiah's Sad Lament
   A. Jesus is the "arm of the Lord"
      1. The presence of God revealed
      2. The power of God demonstrated

   B. Jesus is not accepted or recognized by His people
      1. Who has believed our reports?
      2. To whom has the arm of the Lord been revealed?

Conclusion

10

Great Advent Prophecies: His Birthplace

Micah 5:2 and Matthew 2:5–6

Centuries before Jesus was born, His birthplace was identified and His special character spelled out.

I. The Place of the Messiah's Birth
   A. A suggestive name
      1. Bethlehem ("house of bread")
      2. Ephrathah ("fruitfulness")
   B. A humble location ("little among the thousands of Judah")
      1. Bethlehem was a small town, not a large city
      2. Bethlehem probably had under 1,000 population
   C. A familiar prophecy
      1. In connection with the visit of the wise men (Matt. 2:5–6)
      2. In connection with Jesus' appearance at the feast (John 7)
   D. A remarkable fulfillment
      1. Mary and Joseph
      2. Caesar Augustus (Luke 2:1)
II. The Nature of the Messiah's Rule
   A. He is a ruler, being the Son of David
   B. He is a ruler, being the Son of God
   C. He is a ruler who feeds His flock (v.4)
   D. He is a ruler bringing eventual world peace (v.5)
III. The History of the Messiah's Life
   A. He is from of old
      1. Implies His preexistence
      2. Implies His previous manifestations
         a. To Abraham at the oaks of Mamre
         b. To Jacob at Peniel
         c. To many others throughout Old Testament history
         d. "Before Abraham was, I am"
   B. He is from everlasting

1. Suggests His deity
2. Suggests His eternal existence
3. Jesus is God in the flesh

Conclusion

O holy child of Bethlehem, descend to us, we pray,
Cast out our sin, and enter in; be born in us today.
We hear the Christmas angels the great glad tidings tell;
O come to us, abide with us, our Lord Emmanuel.

11

That Beautiful Name

Matthew 1:21

Jesus came in order to save His people from their sins.

I. **A Name Revealed by an Angel**
   A. It relieved the heart of Joseph regarding Mary
   B. It assured him of the supernatural character of Mary's child
   C. It gave him the honor of naming the child

II. **A Name Understood from Scripture**
   A. "Jesus" is the Greek name for the Hebrew "Joshua"
   B. "Joshua" means "the Lord is salvation"
   C. Joshua is an Old Testament-type of Christ

III. **A Name Indicative of Christ's Saving Work**
   A. Salvation from sin
      1. Not just deliverance from Roman oppression
      2. This is the highest form of salvation
   B. Human race is lost
      1. We don't throw life preservers to sunbathers on the beach
      2. We throw life preservers to people who are drowning
      3. So God sent His life preserver to people who are drowning
         a. People are lost
         b. People are drowning in the sea of sin

IV. **A Name Designed for His People**
   A. Salvation is not for everyone

13

    B. It is only for His people
        1. This implies election
        2. But the gospel is open to all who repent and believe
        3. You can be one of "His people"

Conclusion

12

How Wise Men Listen to God

Matthew 2:1–12

The wise men listened to God in various ways which God still uses today.

  I. Wise Men Listen to God in Nature (vv.1–2)
    A. The wise men saw a supernatural star
    B. The wise men followed the star
    C. God led the wise men to Jerusalem via this star
    D. God still speaks through nature today
        1. Psalm 19
        2. Psalm 8
        3. Romans 1:20

  II. Wise Men Listen to God in the Scriptures (vv.5–6)
    A. God spoke to the wise men through the prophet
        1. Micah 5:2 was quoted
        2. Prophecy foretold the birthplace of the Messiah
        3. Prophecy spoke of the kingly power of Jesus
    B. God still speaks today through His Word
        1. Bible is the primary means of grace
        2. Bible is the only infallible rule for faith and life

  III. Wise Men Listen to God in His Son (vv.10–11)
    A. Jesus Christ is the Word of God made flesh
    B. The wise men understood who Jesus was
        1. They worshiped Him
        2. They presented Him their gifts
    C. God still speaks today through His Son
        1. His birth and earthly life

        2. His miracles
        3. His teachings
        4. His death and resurrection
 IV. **Wise Men Listen to God through Dreams (v.12)**
    A. The wise men received a dream
    B. Much important revelation has been given through dreams
        1. Jacob and the ladder
        2. Joseph in Egypt
        3. Daniel in Babylon
        4. Peter and the sheet let down from heaven
    C. God can still speak through dreams today
        1. When the subconscious life is yielded to the Lord
        2. When we need special guidance

Conclusion

13

Three Reactions to Christmas

Matthew 2:1–12

People responded to the birth of Christ in different ways.

I. **Herod Was Troubled (v.3)**
   A. He was afraid of a potential rival to his throne
   B. His alarm spread to others ("all Jerusalem with him")
   C. His fear finally led to the massacre of the infants
   D. Many people today are troubled by Christmas
        1. If they see Christ as a potential rival to the throne of their lives
        2. If they recognize what the lordship of Christ really means
        3. If they hear the challenge of discipleship and cross-bearing
II. **Jewish Religious Leaders Were Indifferent (vv.4–6)**
    A. Herod inquired where the Christ should be born
    B. Religious leaders gave him the correct answer

    1. They quoted prophecy
    2. They pointed to Bethlehem
  C. But the religious leaders refused to see for themselves
  D. Many people react indifferently to the Christmas message
    1. Non-Christian Americans celebrate Christmas without Christ
    2. They do not care to go to church to find out what it is all about
III. **Wise Men Reacted with Worship (v.11)**
  A. They fell down at His feet in reverence
  B. They offered Him their gifts
    1. Gold
    2. Frankincense
    3. Myrrh
  C. True believers will always respond to Christmas with praise and thanksgiving
    1. They will sing meaningfully
    2. They will pray thankfully
    3. They will offer their gifts generously
    4. They will worship heartily

Conclusion
How do you respond and react to Christmas?

14

Why the Wise Men Were Wise

Matthew 2:1–12

The wise men demonstrated their wisdom in various ways.

I. **The Wisdom in Their Question (v.2)**
  A. It revealed an awakened interest in their hearts
  B. It revealed an ancient belief from the past
    1. The supernatural nature of the star
      a. The prophecy of Balaam in Numbers 24
      b. The prophecies of Daniel
    2. The birth of a great King

C. It revealed an admitted ignorance in their minds
    1. They did not know
    2. They asked questions
    3. A wise person does not necessarily have all the answers
    4. Rather, a wise person is a questioning person
  D. It revealed an avowed motive in their wills
    1. They came to worship Him
    2. They came to worship a King
II. **The Wisdom in Their Activity**
  A. They received a sign, the star
    1. They did not just admire it
    2. They did not just study it
  B. They acted on the sign they were given
    1. They travelled hundreds of miles
    2. They followed the star
    3. They persevered in following despite discouragements
      a. The star seems to have disappeared for a while
      b. The babe was not in Jerusalem and no one seemed to care
      c. Wise people do not give up in a hurry
III. **The Wisdom in Their Example**
  A. They rejoiced (v.10)
  B. They worshiped (v.11)
  C. They gave gifts (v.11)
    1. Gold
    2. Frankincense
    3. Myrrh
  D. They listened to God (v.12)
    1. Warned by a dream
    2. They went back home another way

Conclusion

15

Home for the Holidays?

Matthew 2:13–23

Jesus Christ and His parents were forced to flee to the land of Egypt because His life was in danger.

I. **Fact of Satanic Hatred**
   A. Herod hated any possible rival to his throne
   B. Herod attempted to kill Jesus
   C. Herod destroyed all the male babies in Bethlehem
   D. Herod was a tool in the hand of Satan (cf. Rev. 12:3–5)

II. **Fact of Divine Protection**
   A. Joseph's dreams
   B. Joseph's obedience
   C. Joseph's continued dependence upon God

III. **Fact of Fulfilled Prophecy**
   A. Verse 15 from Hosea 11:1
   B. Verse 18 from Jeremiah 31:15
   C. Verse 23 from Isaiah 11:1?

IV. **Fact of Lonely Rejection**
   A. Jesus was rejected
      1. By Herod
      2. By His own people
         a. Isaiah 53
         b. John 1:11–13
      3. By many people today
   B. Christians can sometimes feel rejected and lonely
      1. By family
      2. By the church
      3. By God
   C. Jesus identifies with you in your feelings at Christmas

Conclusion

16

The Forerunner's Mother

Luke 1:5–6; 24–25; 39–45

Elizabeth praised God and blessed Mary when she heard the news that Mary was to be the mother of the Messiah.

I. **Background Information**
   A. Her name: Elizabeth
   B. Her family: House of Aaron (v.5)
   C. Her marriage: to Zechariah, a priest
   D. Her disgrace: she was barren (v.7)

II. Elizabeth's Faith
   A. They were both righteous before the Lord (v.6)
   B. They kept all the commandments of the Lord (v.7)

III. Elizabeth's Special Insights
   A. From her husband; she was to have a child
   B. From the babe leaping in her womb
   C. From the Holy Spirit
      1. The miracle of the virgin birth (v.42)
      2. The supernatural child of Mary (v.43)
      3. The quality of Mary's faith (v.45)
         a. It was simple trust and acceptance
         b. Contrast with Zechariah's doubt and unbelief

IV. Elizabeth's Humility
   A. Toward God
      1. She hid herself five months (v.24)
      2. This was a time for spiritual reflection
   B. Toward Mary
      1. She honored Mary above herself (v.43)
      2. She showed no jealousy that Mary's child would be greater than her own

V. Elizabeth's Prophecy
   A. Mary was to be blessed (v.45)
   B. The fulfillment (babe) would be born
   C. This was the confirmation Mary needed
      1. Mary came to share her condition with Elizabeth
      2. But Elizabeth supernaturally knew about it already
         a. This confirmed Mary's faith
         b. It caused Mary to break forth into song (vv.45–55)

Conclusion

17

Fear Not, Zechariah!

Luke 1:12–13

Zechariah was afraid of the angel who announced the birth of his son.

I. A Father's Fear
   A. Fear of the angel in the temple

    B. Fear of the unknown
    C. Fear of the unseen spirit world
II. The Angel's Answer to the Father's Fear
    A. God hears your prayer (v.13b)
        1. Zechariah had prayed many times for children
        2. God had not granted that request
        3. God answers prayer in His own time
        4. Don't give up on prayer
    B. God will give you a special son
        1. He will be great in the sight of the Lord
        2. He will be in control of himself
            a. No wine
            b. No strong drink
        3. He will be filled with the Spirit
        4. He will be a missionary to his people
        5. He will prepare the way for the Messiah
    C. God will turn your fear to joy (v.14)

Conclusion

18

The Christmas Angel

Luke 1:19, 26, 28–37

Gabriel was the obedient angel of God sent on several different occasions to bring God's message to His people.

I. **His Name**
    A. Gabriel
    B. Meaning "man of God"
    C. Importance of being a "man of God"
II. **His Appearance**
    A. Angels normally are invisible
    B. Gabriel came visibly
    C. Angels can sometimes take on visible appearance
III. **His Position**
    A. In the presence of God
        1. Intimate knowledge of God and His will
        2. Christians should also live in the presence of God

           B. I stand in the presence of God
              1. Not just resting, abiding, living in presence of God
              2. He stands in the presence of God
                 a. Standing indicates readiness to serve
                 b. Standing indicates readiness to listen and obey
   IV. His Task
       A. He is sent by God
       B. He is sent by God to speak
       C. He is sent by God to speak good news
   V. His Message
       A. To Daniel (Dan. 8:16–17; 9:20–23)
       B. To Zechariah (fatherhood in his old age)
          1. Assurance (v.13; cf. v.11—by altar of incense)
          2. Promise (vv.13–15)
          3. Blessing (vv.16–17)
          4. Judgment (v.20)
       C. To Mary (motherhood by the Holy Spirit)
          1. Greeting (v.28)
          2. Assurance (v.30)
          3. Promise (vv.31–35)
          4. Confirmation (vv.37–38)
Conclusion

19

The Miraculous Birth

Luke 1:35

The miracle of the virgin birth has great significance for believers today.

  I. **The Fact of the Virgin Birth**
     A. It was positively announced by the angel
     B. It was humbly accepted by Mary
     C. It was gloriously confirmed by Elizabeth
 II. **The Miracle of the Virgin Birth**
     A. It is in the conception, not the birth
        1. The real miracle of Christmas was nine months before Christmas

        2. Jesus' birth at Christmas was normal in every way
    B. It is in what happened to God, not to Mary
        1. Mary's miracle has received all the attention
        2. But the real miracle was the incarnation of God's Son
III. **The Significance of the Virgin Birth**
    A. It highlights Christ's purity and sinlessness ("that holy thing")
    B. It highlights Christ's deity ("Son of God")
Conclusion

20

The "Magnificat"

Luke 1:46–55

Mary's song praised God for the miracle of Christmas and what that miracle meant for her and her people.

I. **The Inspiration for This Song**
    A. It was not the angel's announcement
    B. It was rather the confirmation received from Elizabeth
II. **The Background for This Song**
    A. Explanation of Hebrew poetry
        1. No rhyme or meter
        2. Parallelism and repetition of thought patterns
    B. Biblical language
        1. Resemblances to the song of Hannah (I Sam. 2)
        2. Thoughts from the Psalms
III. **The Song Itself**
    A. Stanza 1 (vv.46–48)
        1. Mary's praise to God for the high honor given her
        2. Mary's recognition of her own need of salvation
            a. There is no "immaculate conception" here
            b. Mary was a sinner in need of a Savior
        3. Mary's humility
            a. She speaks of her low estate
            b. She calls herself the handmaid of the Lord
        4. Mary's place in history
            a. All generations shall call her blessed

        b. She is blessed, but not to be idolized
    B. Stanza 2 (vv.49–50)
        1. Praise to God for His power(virgin birth)
        2. Praise to God for His holiness
        3. Praise to God for His mercy
    C. Stanza 3 (vv.51–53)
        1. There is a complete reversal of all human values
        2. This is exemplified in Mary and Elizabeth themselves
    D. Stanza 4 (vv.54–55)
        1. God's faithfulness to His covenant promises
            a. God has remembered His people
            b. God has not forgotten His ancient promises
        2. God will remain faithful today
Conclusion

21

The "Benedictus"

Luke 1:68–79

Zechariah sang a song of praise to God after his speech was restored. He thanked God for the gift of salvation through the coming Messiah.

I. **The Background for This Song**
   A. The angel's announcement
   B. Zechariah's unbelief
   C. Zechariah's loss of speech
   D. Zechariah's speech restored
   E. Zechariah's praise to God

II. **The Introduction to This Song**
   A. He was filled with the Holy Spirit
   B. He prophesied
   C. He did not boast about his newborn son
   D. He brought the glory to God

III. **Zechariah's Song Itself**
   A. Stanza 1—Zechariah praises God for the Messiah
        1. Praise for God's mercy
        2. Praise for the messianic deliverance

        a. Jesus is a horn of salvation
        b. Deliverance is spiritual, not earthly
     3. Purpose of deliverance
     4. Outcome of deliverance
  B. Stanza 2—the role of John the Baptist
     1. To prepare the way for the Messiah
     2. To anticipate the Messiah
        a. Messiah will bring light to those in darkness
        b. Messiah will bring peace to men

Conclusion

Unbelief produces no great Christmas music. Unbelief leads to silence. Only faith produces the songs of Christmas.

22

The Dayspring from on High

Luke 1:79

Zechariah, in the closing stanza of his "Benedictus," referred to the coming of the Messiah as a light entering into a dark world.

I. The People Visited
   A. Those that sit in darkness (sin)
      1. Darkness of Judaism
      2. Darkness of paganism
      3. Darkness of Greek philosophy
      4. Darkness of sin
   B. Those that sit in the shadow of death
      1. They are hopeless. Sitting implies no longer looking for a way out of troubles; they are resigned to their fate
      2. They are living with death hovering over them
         a. Death of sin
         b. Death of the body
         c. Death of hell

II. **The Symbolic Coming**
    A. It is like morning daybreak, the rise of a new day
        1. The Messiah would usher in a new age
        2. The new age is characterized as light
           a. cf. Malachi 4:2
           b. cf. Isaiah 9:2
           c. cf. Isaiah 60:1
           d. cf. II Samuel 23:4
    B. It is unlike morning daybreak
        1. At daybreak the sun rises out of the horizon, gradually
        2. Christ shall arise from "on high"
           a. Christ is the Son of God
           b. Emphasis on His deity
III. **The Blessings Granted**
    A. Knowledge of salvation in remission of sin (v.77)
    B. Guidance of our feet into the way of peace
IV. **The Divine Motivation (the tender mercy of our God)**
Conclusion

23

The Faces of the Shepherds

Luke 2:8–20

The shepherds hurried to Bethlehem in order to see the infant, and then returned glorifying and praising God.

    I. **Frightened Eyes (vv.8–9)**
        A. The glory of the Lord shone around them
        B. The shepherds were afraid
   II. **Listening Ears (vv.10–14)**
        A. They heard a message
        B. They heard a song
  III. **Determined Mouths (vv.15–16a)**
        A. Let us go even unto Bethlehem
        B. They were determined to see what had happened
        C. They came with haste

IV. Happy Smiles (vv.16b–20)
   A. At the manger
   B. Back at their work
      1. They praised God
      2. They glorified Him
V. Witnessing Lips (vv.17–18)
   A. They made known what they had heard
   B. They made known what they had seen

Conclusion

24

The Message Heard by the Shepherds

Luke 2:8–11

The shepherds near Bethlehem heard a marvelous message from the angels concerning the birth of Christ.

I. Who Were the Shepherds?
   A. Their history
   B. Their reputation
   C. Their culture
   D. Their occupation
   E. Their faith
II. Why Were the Shepherds Afraid?
   A. An angel appearance
   B. The shining glory of the Lord
III. What Did the Shepherds Hear?
   A. Fear not
      1. This shows the Lord's tender concern
      2. This shows the Lord's knowledge of their feelings
   B. Message of good news for all
      1. The Savior is born
      2. The Savior is Christ
      3. The Savior is the Lord

C. An anthem of praise to God
      1. Glory to God in the highest
      2. Peace on earth to men in whom God is well-pleased

Conclusion

25

Fear Not, Shepherds

Luke 2:9–10

On Christmas night the shepherds were afraid when they saw the glory of the Lord shining around about them, but the angel's message answered that fear.

   I. Who Were the Shepherds?
      A. Guardians of the sheep
      B. Simple and humble men
      C. Honored recipients of the Christmas message
  II. Why Were the Shepherds Afraid?
      A. The glory of the Lord shone around them
      B. A fear of God's glory and greatness
      C. A fear of the unknown
      D. A sense of sin and unworthiness
 III. What Is the Answer to the Shepherds' Fear?
      A. Fear not!
      B. Angels came to bring good news
      C. Good news of great joy
      D. The Messiah's birth—unto you is born
      E. The Messiah's birthplace—in the city of David
      F. The Messiah's work—a Savior
      G. The Messiah's natures
         1. He is Christ—the anointed one
         2. He is the Lord—divinity
      H. This message is for all men—unto you
  IV. What Fears Do You Face Today?
      A. Fears are common to all people
      B. The gospel is still the answer to your fear

Conclusion

26
The Sign Received by the Shepherds

Luke 2:12

The swaddling clothes was the sign by which the shepherds could identify God's Son.

I. **The Necessity of the Sign**
   A. Not to identify the child
   B. Rather to confirm the truth of the message

II. **The Novelty of the Sign**
   A. The gift—a baby
   B. The gift-wrapping—swaddling clothes
   C. The package—lying in a manger

III. **The News in the Sign**
   A. Poverty
      1. cf. II Corinthians 8:9
      2. cf. Philippians 2:5-8
   B. Rejection
      1. cf. Luke 2:7
      2. cf. John 1:11-13

Conclusion

27
The Paradox of Christ's Coming: Peace or Sword?

Luke 2:14b and Matthew 10:34-36

Christ came to create peace on the vertical level between God and man, but that new relationship with God can create tension and even hostility on the horizontal level.

I. **Christ Came to Bring Peace to the World**
   A. Peace was a major part of the angel's song on Christmas night
   B. Peace was vertical rather than horizontal
      1. Not "peace on earth, good will toward men"
      2. Rather "peace among men in whom God is well-pleased"
   C. Peace with God leads to peace among men
      1. Angels sang about "peace among men"
      2. Harmony between Jew and Gentile (Eph. 2:14–15)

II. **Christ Came Not to Bring Peace but a Sword**
   A. The mystery of this statement
   B. The explanation of this statement
      1. Christ creates divisions between people in realm of ideas and thoughts
         a. Different responses to His claims
         b. Different responses to His call for a unique lifestyle
         c. Different responses to His challenge for discipleship
      2. Spiritual conflict can lead to use of force
         a. Jesus spoke in text of "the sword"
         b. Many Christians have died for their faith
   C. The application of this statement
      1. Within the family
         a. Father and son
         b. Mother and daughter
         c. Mother-in-law and daughter-in-law
      2. Within the church (context)
         True Christians are always a threat to nominal Christians

III. **Christ Creates a New Peace on a New Level**
   A. Not necessarily on national and family level
   B. Rather within the fellowship of true believers
      1. Peace with God
      2. Peace with our fellow Christians

Conclusion

28

The Child Found by the Shepherds

Luke 2:15–16

The obedience of the shepherds led them quickly to the manger.

I. **Their Reflections (v.15a)**
   A. The angels went away from them
      1. Was it only a dream?
      2. Was it only an illusion?
   B. The shepherds thought about the supernatural occurrence they had witnessed

II. **Their Decision (v.15b)**
   A. Let us go to Bethlehem
   B. Let us see what has come to pass
   C. Let us see what the Lord has revealed
      1. They recognized the hand of God in the angelic visit
      2. They accepted divine revelation

III. **Their Haste (v.16a)**
   A. Their haste reveals their excitement
   B. Their haste reveals their faith
   C. Their haste reveals their joy

IV. **Their Reward (v.16b)**
   A. They found Mary and Joseph
   B. They found the babe lying in the manger

Conclusion

29

The Witness of the Shepherds

Luke 2:17–18

A true understanding of the Christmas message leads to sharing that message with others.

I. Who Are These Witnesses?
   A. Negatively
      1. They are not the intelligentsia
      2. They are not biblical scholars
      3. They are not full-time mission workers
   B. Positively
      1. They were shepherds
      2. They were laborers
      3. They were lay people

II. What Was Their Witness?
   A. It was a testimony of an experience with Christ
      1. They told what they saw (v.17a)
      2. It was their experience, not someone else's
   B. It was a verbal or word testimony
   C. It was a testimony concerning the person of Christ
      1. They made known the saying spoken to them
      2. They made known who Jesus was
         a. A Savior (v.11)
         b. Christ (v.11)
         c. The Lord (v.11)

III. How Do You Witness?
   A. Many Christians have problems with this
      1. They assume it means ringing doorbells
      2. They assume it means handing out tracts everywhere
      3. They assume it means memorizing many texts and "spiritual laws"
      4. They assume it means going to jails, hospitals, etc.
   B. Real witnessing is much more natural and spontaneous
      1. It is making known what has happened to you
      2. It is making known what you have learned from God

C. Witnessing is a Christian's responsibility
      1. We cannot keep Christ and Christmas to ourselves
      2. If our experience with Christ is real, we will share it
IV. **The Response to the Shepherds' Witness**
   A. All who heard it wondered
   B. It does not say that they all became believers
   C. Witnessing is simply sowing seed, not necessarily leading everyone to Christ

Conclusion

30

The Worship Expressed by the Shepherds

Luke 2:20

The shepherds glorified and praised God for the gift of Christmas.

I. **The Shepherds Returned to Their Work**
   A. They watched over their flocks by night
      1. It was dull and boring work
      2. They were exposed to the elements of nature
      3. It was the "graveyard shift"
      4. It was work requiring constant alertness
   B. The shepherds had to return to do this work after seeing Jesus
      1. It could have been a letdown for them
      2. It could have led to complaining and bitterness
II. **The Shepherds Had a New Attitude as They Went Back to Work**
   A. They glorified God
   B. They praised God
   C. Their work was transformed by seeing Christ
III. **The Shepherds Had a New Motivation**
   A. All the things they had heard
      1. The message of the angels
      2. The song of the angels

    B. All the things they had seen
        1. The baby in the manger
        2. The swaddling clothes
    C. The evidence of God's truth ("even as it was spoken unto them")
IV. **Application**
    A. Have you met Christ?
    B. Are you praising and glorifying God?
    C. What is your attitude toward your work?
        1. You can have a new attitude
        2. Christ can transform your dull and ordinary experiences too

Conclusion

31

The Problem of Post-Christmas Blues

Luke 2:22–39

Mary and Joseph experienced many of the situations which could have caused a feeling of post-Christmas depression.

I. **The Causes of Potential Depression**
    A. Loneliness
        1. Mary and Joseph were far from home and family
        2. They were forced by circumstances not to return home for a long time
            a. Forty days until the purification in Jerusalem
            b. Several months until the visit of the wise men
            c. Several years in Egypt
    B. Frustration
        1. Caesar Augustus' enrollment for tax purposes
        2. No room for them in the inn
    C. Poverty
        1. Mary and Joseph had no money
        2. Their sacrifice in the temple indicates their poverty (cf. v.24)

            D. Prophecy (vv.34–35)
                1. This child is set for the rise and fall of many in Israel
                2. A sword shall pierce your own soul also
    II. The Cure for Post-Christmas Blues
            A. An attitude of praise and worship
                1. Shepherds and wise men
                2. Simeon and Anna
            B. A new sense of peace (Simeon, v.29)
            C. A new sense of obedience (Simeon)
            D. A new sense of outreach
                1. Simeon recognized Christ as a light to the Gentiles
                2. Anna herself spoke of Him to everyone (v.38)
Conclusion

32

The "Nunc Dimittis"

Luke 2:29–32

The song of Simeon was the song with the widest horizons, for it spoke of the Messiah's mission to the Gentile world as well as to the Jews.

   I. The Occasion for This Song
        A. Mary's purification according to Levitical law
        B. Jesus' parents came to the temple for this purpose
        C. The offering they brought indicated their poverty
  II. The Singer of This Song
        A. Simeon was an old man
        B. He was righteous (v.25)
        C. He was devout (v.25)
        D. He looked for the consolation of Israel (v.25)
        E. He was filled with the Spirit (v.25)
            1. Spirit gave him revelation (v.25)
            2. Spirit gave him daily direction (v.27)
            3. Spirit gave him inspiration (vv.29–32)
 III. The Song Itself
        A. Simeon's death announcement (v.29)
            1. His long wait is over

    2. Death is a departure
    3. Believers can die in peace
  B. Reasons for Simeon's gratitude (vv.30–31)
    1. He had seen God's salvation
       a. Note his prophecy in verse 34
       b. He saw this child as the suffering and dying Messiah
    2. God has made His salvation known to all people
  C. The Messiah's work (v.32)
    1. A light for revelation to the Gentiles
    2. A light for Israel's glory

Conclusion
Christmas is a time for the joy of singing.
Christmas songs arise from godly hearts full of faith.
Christmas ought to lead us to think of outreach, missions, and evangelism as it did for Simeon.

33

The Miracle of Christmas

John 1:14

The incarnation of the Son of God was the greatest miracle of Christmas.

I. **The Incarnation ("The Word was made flesh")**
   A. The meaning of the word *incarnation*
   B. The impossibility of human achievement (cf. Dan. 2:11)
   C. The universal longing for it (Acts 14:11)
   D. The divine Word
     1. From the beginning (v.1)
     2. With God
     3. Active in creation (v.3)
     4. Is the light (v.4)
     5. Rejected by men (vv.11–12)
   E. The Word was made flesh
     1. What is flesh?
     2. It is human nature
        a. Weakness

  b. Fatigue
  c. Sorrow
  d. Suffering
II. Identification
 A. With us ("He dwelt among us")
  1. Meaning "he tabernacled among us"
  2. He was no apparition or make-believe person
  3. He was a real person who lived a real life
 B. With God ("We beheld His glory")
  1. The manger tends to hide His glory
  2. But the glory is there
   a. Shepherds—the glory of the Lord shone round them
   b. Wise Men—saw a glorious star
  3. Special reference here to the experience on the Mount of Transfiguration
III. Intervention ("He is full of grace and truth")
 A. Sin in the human race made this necessary
 B. Son of God intervened in human history
  1. He brought us grace
  2. He brought us truth

Conclusion

34

Why Jesus Came

John 3:16 and Ephesians 3:18

Christmas is a revelation of the four dimensions of God's love.

I. The Breadth of God's Love
 A. God so loved
 B. God so loved the world
II. The Length of God's Love (to what lengths will it go?)
 A. God gave His Son
 B. God gave His only-begotten Son
III. The Depth of God's Love
 A. God's love saves us from perishing

    B. God's love saves us only through faith
    C. God's love is available to all (whosoever)
IV. The Height of God's Love
    A. God gave us life
    B. God gave us eternal life

Conclusion

35

The Paradox of Christ's Coming: To Judge or Not to Judge

John 12:47 and John 9:39

Christ came into the world to save sinners and not to judge them, yet there is an inevitable judgment that takes place whenever the good news is preached.

  I. Jesus Came Not to Judge the World (12:47)
    A. The first coming was for salvation (cf. 3:17)
    B. The second coming will be for judgment
        1. Apostle's Creed. He will come again to judge living and dead
        2. II Corinthians 5:10
  II. Jesus Came into the World for Judgment (9:39)
    A. The occasion which called forth this comment
        1. The healing of the blind man
        2. He was healed physically
        3. He was healed spiritually
    B. The basic principle stated
        1. Christ did not come for judgment
        2. But a judgment was an inevitable result of His coming
           a. Christ points out sin
           b. Christ tests the true and the false

            c. Christ forces a person to take a position
            d. Christ never leaves us the way He found us
                1) The gospel is sometimes a savor of life unto life (II Cor. 2:16)
                2) The gospel is sometimes a savor of death unto death (II Cor. 2:16)
    C. The basic principle illustrated
        1. The blind man received life
        2. The Pharisees were hardened in their unbelief (vv.40–41)
            a. Reject Christ and you bring judgment on yourself
            b. Reject salvation and you are judged already (3:18)
            c. The Pharisees were the ones who were truly blind
III. **Resolving the Paradox**
    A. Christmas means salvation and not judgment
    B. Judgment follows inevitably wherever the Christmas gospel is preached
Conclusion

36

The Universal Longing

Acts 14:11

The universal desire in the hearts of all pagan people everywhere was to have their gods come down to them in the likeness of men, but only at Bethlehem did the longing of men actually happen.

I. **The Miracle (vv.8–10)**
    A. Miracle of healing
    B. A miracle of faith-healing
II. **The Myth (vv.11–13)**
    A. Their belief in incarnation
        1. cf. Acts 8:10
        2. cf. Acts 28:6
    B. Their belief in divine power
    C. Their belief in fellowship with the gods

III. The Message (vv.13–18)
  A. We are not gods
  B. We are men who bring the gospel of God
     1. God is the creator
     2. God is revealed in nature
     3. God is best revealed in His Son
        a. He came down to earth not just to do miracles
        b. He came down to suffer and die
        c. He came down to deliver us from sin

Conclusion

The heart of the Christian message is the Incarnation. Men have always longed for this. It actually happened at Bethlehem.

37

What Time Is It?

Romans 13:11–14

It is time to awake out of sleep and live a consistent Christian life because of the nearness of our salvation.

I. Time to Wake Up
  A. Salvation is nearer now than when we first believed
  B. The night is far gone and the day is at hand

II. Time to Break Up
  A. Break up with the works of darkness
  B. Put on the armor of light
  C. Live a consistent Christian life
     1. No drunkenness and revelry
     2. No debauchery and licentiousness

III. Time to Make Up
  A. Christians must put aside quarreling
  B. Christians must put aside their jealousy

IV. Time to Shape Up
  A. Shape up by putting on the Lord Jesus Christ
  B. Shape up by refusing to make provision for the flesh

Conclusion

38

Advent Hope

Romans 15:4-13

One of the keynotes of the Advent season is hope, a quality which unites Jews and Gentiles together in a common bond of faith and gives rise to united praise, joy, and peace.

I. **The Source of Hope**
   A. The Scriptures (v.4)
   B. The Holy Spirit (v.13b)

II. **The Blessings of Hope**
   A. The blessing of unity
      1. Of the same mind with one another (v.5)
      2. Of one accord (v.6)
      3. With one mouth (v.6)
      4. Accept one another (v.7)
      5. Jews and Gentiles in one church (vv.8-12)
         a. Jews glorify God among the Gentiles (v.9)
         b. Gentiles rejoice with the Jews (v.10)
         c. All Jews and Gentiles praise God together (v.11)
         d. Christ reigns over both Jews and Gentiles (v.12)
   B. The blessing of joy (v.13a)
   C. The blessing of peace (v.13a)

III. **The Supreme Example of Hope**
   A. Christ pleased not Himself (v.3)
      1. He took our reproaches upon Himself
      2. Christ is the primary example of hope
   B. According to Christ Jesus (v.5)
   C. Even as Christ also received you (v.7)

Conclusion

39

In the Fullness of Time

Galatians 4:4–5

Jesus came at Christmas in order to redeem us and adopt us into the family of God.

I. **Christ's Coming**
   A. The time of His coming (in the fullness of time)
      1. The date of Christmas is unknown
      2. December 25 is a date with pagan origins
      3. Christ came in the fullness of time
      4. The world was ripe for His coming
         a. The political situation
         b. The moral and spiritual situation
         c. The cultural situation
   B. The manner of His coming
      1. God sent forth His Son
      2. This implies Christ's preexistence
         a. Jesus did not begin His life at Bethlehem
         b. Jesus had lived from eternity with the Father
   C. The humility of His coming
      1. He was born of a woman
         a. He was born of Mary in Bethlehem
         b. He identifies Himself with the human race
      2. He was born under the law
         a. Not because He had sinned
         b. This is part of His identification with our sin
            1) He became a curse for us (Gal. 3:13)
            2) He submitted to the law throughout His life
            3) He kept the law

II. **The Purpose of Christ's Coming**
   A. Initial purpose—to redeem us
      1. We were condemned by the law
      2. Christ took our condemnation
      3. Christ went to the cross to redeem us
   B. Ultimate purpose—our adoption as sons
      1. Redemption is only a legal act
      2. Adoption is an act of love

a. We are now children of God
  b. We have fellowship with God
  c. We are heirs of eternal life

Conclusion

40

A Lesson in Humility

Philippians 2:5–8

Jesus came into this world in order to teach a lesson in humility.

I. **What Is the Mind of Christ?**
   A. He existed in the form of God
      1. His preexistence
      2. His divinity
   B. He did not count equality with God as something to be grasped
      1. He emptied Himself
         a. Meaning of this "emptying"
         b. Jesus did not cling to His rights as God
      2. He took the form of a servant
         a. His servant ministry
         b. Washing the disciples' feet
         c. He came not to be ministered unto
         d. He came to minister
      3. He was made in the likeness of men
         a. He did not give up His deity
         b. He added humanity to His deity
      4. He humbled Himself
         a. His lowly birth
         b. His peasant parents
      5. He became obedient even unto death
         a. His obedience
         b. His terrible death on the cross

II. **Have This Mind in You Which Was also in Christ Jesus**
   A. Christmas is a lesson in humility
   B. Christmas cost God His Son

C. Christmas will also cost us something
      1. We will also empty ourselves
         a. of pride
         b. of self-righteousness
      2. We will also be servants to others
      3. We will also humble ourselves

Conclusion

APPENDIX

Five Series of Advent Messages

On the following pages five series of messages are provided for use in the Christmas season. Each series contains at least one sermon idea—text, theme, and title—for every Sunday in Advent.

1. The Night of Miracles
Advent 1
Text: Luke 1:33
Theme: The first great miracle of Christmas was the virgin birth, beautifully and tastefully described by Gabriel to Mary
Title: THE MIRACULOUS BIRTH
Advent 2
Text: Matthew 2:2

Theme: The appearance of a supernatural star was used by God to lead the wise men to Bethlehem.
Title: THE MIRACULOUS STAR

Advent 3
Text: Matthew 2:6
Theme: The amazing fulfillment of prophecy was a miracle in the hand of God.
Title: THE AMAZING FULFILLMENT OF PROPHECY

Advent 4
Text: Luke 2:9–14
Theme: God miraculously sent angels to the shepherds on Christmas night to inform them of the news of the Savior's birth.
Title: THE MIRACULOUS ANGELS

Christmas Eve or Christmas Day
Text: John 1:14
Theme: The incarnation of the Son of God was the greatest miracle of Christmas.
Title: THE GREATEST MIRACLE OF ALL!

Sunday After Christmas
Text: Matthew 4:23–25
Theme: Jesus Christ carried on both a healing and a teaching ministry in all Galilee.
Title: THE MIRACLE WORKER

Second Sunday After Christmas
Text: Acts 2:22 and Acts 14:3
Theme: God used the miracles of Jesus as divine proof of our Lord's authority and power and to give credibility to His message.
Title: THE MEANING OF THE MIRACLES

During the Christmas season, a very appropriate cantata for the church choir to sing would be John Peterson's *The Night of Miracles*.

2. Isaiah's Great Christmas Messages

Advent 1
Text: Isaiah 64:4–8
Theme: The longing of Israel was for God to come down and help them in their desolate condition created by sin.
Title: REND THE HEAVENS!

Advent 2
Text: Isaiah 61:1–3 and Luke 4:21
Theme: The Spirit of the Lord equipped Jesus for a caring and sharing ministry.

Title: A SERMON FOR NAZARETH

Advent 3
Text: Isaiah 12:3 and John 4:10
Theme: The Christ came to provide living water which His people would draw from the wells of salvation.
Title: THE WELLS OF SALVATION

Advent 4
Text: Isaiah 25:8, 9
Theme: The Messiah for whom Israel was looking would bring them gladness and salvation while ending death and all its misery forever.
Title: POINSETTIAS AND EASTER LILIES

Christmas Eve or Christmas Day
Text: Isaiah 9:2 and John 8:12
Theme: The Lord Jesus Christ is the light of the world as foretold by the prophets.
Title: THE LIGHT OF THE WORLD

Sunday After Christmas
Text: Isaiah 55:1–7
Theme: Since God offers us a full and free salvation in Jesus Christ, it is fitting that we respond to His call to repent and believe.
Title: THE GOSPEL OF GRACE

New Year's Eve or New Year's Day
Text: Isaiah 26:3, 4
Theme: God keeps us in perfect peace when our minds and hearts are fixed on Him.
Title: HOW TO HAVE PEACE IN THE NEW YEAR!

3. What Child Is This?

Advent 1
Text: Matthew 16:13–16
Theme: The child of Bethlehem is really the Son of the living God.
Title: THIS CHILD IS THE SON OF GOD

Advent 2
Text: Galatians 4:4, 5
Theme: The child of Bethlehem is a real man, having been born of a woman in the fullness of time.
Title: THIS CHILD IS THE SON OF MARY

Advent 3
Text: Zechariah 13:1
Theme: The child of Bethlehem is a fountain for cleansing from sin.

Title: THIS CHILD IS THE CLEANSING FOUNTAIN
Advent 4
Text: Isaiah 9:6
Theme: The child of Bethlehem is the Prince of Peace.
Title: THIS CHILD IS THE PRINCE OF PEACE
Christmas Eve or Christmas Day
Text: Matthew 1:21
Theme: The child of Bethlehem was named Jesus because He would save His people from their sins.
Title: THIS CHILD IS OUR SAVIOR
Sunday After Christmas
Text: Philippians 2:5–11
Theme: The child of Bethlehem lived a little while in humility, but now is the Lord of heaven and earth before whom every knee shall one day bow.
Title: THIS CHILD IS OUR LORD
New Year's Eve or New Year's Day
Text: Matthew 16:27
Theme: The child of Bethlehem is coming again in power and great glory to render to every man according to his deeds.
Title: THIS CHILD IS OUR COMING KING

4. The Ancestry of Our Lord
Advent 1
Text: Genesis 3:15
Theme: The first messianic prophecy in Scripture points us to the future seed of the woman (Eve) who would crush the head of the serpent.
Title: THE SEED OF THE WOMAN
Advent 2
Text: Genesis 22:18
Theme: God promised Abraham that one of his descendants (his seed) would one day bless all of the nations of the world.
Title: THE SEED OF ABRAHAM.
Advent 3
Text: Genesis 49:10
Theme: God promised that ruling authority would belong to Judah and his tribe until the coming of the Messiah, after which kingly authority would belong to Him.
Title: THE SEED OF JUDAH
Advent 4
Text: II Samuel 7:12, 13

Theme: God promised David that a kingdom would be established through his descendants (his seed).
Title: THE SEED OF DAVID

Christmas Eve or Christmas Day
Text: Matthew 1:18–23
Theme: Jesus Christ was conceived by the Holy Spirit and born of the virgin Mary.
Title: THE SEED OF MARY

Sunday After Christmas
Text: Luke 1:35 and Romans 1:3, 4
Theme: The seed of David is also the mighty Son of God, as testified in both His birth and His resurrection.
Title: THE SON OF GOD

5. Shadows at Christmas Time

Advent 1
Text: Luke 1:18
Theme: Zechariah responded to the message of the angels with an expression of doubt and unbelief.
Title: THE SHADOW OF DOUBT

Advent 2
Text: Luke 2:7
Theme: The night Jesus was born, there was no room for Him in the inn.
Title: THE SHADOW OF INSECURITY or NO VACANCY

Advent 3
Text: Luke 2:34, 35
Theme: Simeon prophesied that a sword would pierce Mary's soul.
Title: THE SHADOW OF HEARTBREAK or THE SWORD THROUGH MARY'S SOUL

Advent 4
Text: Matthew 2:13–18
Theme: Herod tried to destroy the infant Jesus by killing all the male children in Bethlehem.
Title: THE SHADOW OF DEATH or RACHEL CRYING FOR HER CHILDREN

Christmas Eve or Christmas Day
Text: Revelation 12:1–6
Theme: This "behind the scenes" picture of Christmas shows Satan trying constantly to destroy the line of Christ and prevent the Savior from coming into the world.
Title: THE SHADOW OF SATAN or THE GREAT RED DRAGON

Sunday After Christmas
Text: Matthew 1:21
Theme: Jesus Christ came into the world in order to save His people from their sins.
Title: THE SHADOW OF THE CROSS

New Year's Eve
Text: Revelation 21:1–4
Theme: In heaven God will dwell with His people forever, removing all the sorrows and sufferings of this life.
Title: WHEN THE SHADOWS VANISH AWAY.